# Time Billionaire
KG NEWMAN

Bainbridge Island Press

# TIME BILLIONAIRE

# KG NEWMAN

Bainbridge Island Press
*Bainbridge Island, WA*

Time Billionaire by KG Newman
Copyright © 2024
All rights reserved

No portion of this book may be reproduced in any form without written permission from the publisher or author, except as permitted by U.S. copyright law.

Published in 2024 by Bainbridge Island Press
Bainbridge Island, WA
https://bainbridgeisland.press

Printed in the United States of America

ISBN: 978-1-961451-08-7
Library of Congress Control Number: 2024948271

Cover & Book Design: Ben Rockwood

9 8 7 6 5 4 3 2 1

*For all the moments we neglect to put in our pocket*

# Also by KG Newman

While Dreaming of Diamonds in Wintertime (2013)

Selfish Never Get Their Own (2016)

Husband Father Failure (2019)

The Smell of Campfire (2022)

# Contents

## I   THE IDENTITY CLOCK

| | |
|---|---|
| FISTFULS OF GRAVEL BENEATH OUR FEET | 6 |
| THE WATCH WAR | 7 |
| TIME BILLIONAIRE | 8 |
| OFF-DAY DEMANDS | 9 |
| THE FELLED PINE TREES SPEAK | 10 |
| BLACKOUT | 11 |
| EASY TIME | 12 |
| RE-BEING PETER PAN | 13 |
| THE SHEARING | 14 |
| IT'S OKAY EVERYTHING'S FINE | 15 |
| COTTONWOOD SUMMER | 16 |
| SINGE ME | 17 |
| AMBROSIA FORMULA | 18 |
| MY CRETACEOUS PERIOD | 19 |
| THE GALLOPING FIELDS | 20 |
| FREEFALL | 21 |

## II   THE HEART CLOCK

| | |
|---|---|
| BECOMING WOODCHIPS | 24 |
| OUR DE-EXTINCTION | 25 |
| MY PERSISTENCE OF MEMORY, EXPLAINED | 26 |
| OUR ETERNALISM | 27 |
| THE FRUIT MATRIX | 28 |
| TINY REPRIEVES | 29 |
| BUNDLED TIME | 30 |
| THREADS | 31 |
| COLLATERAL ORGANS | 32 |
| ON MY MIND | 33 |
| BURNING HANDS | 34 |
| SPORES | 35 |
| ANNULUS | 36 |
| INFINITY TEA | 37 |
| THE TAN LINES ON OUR WRISTS | 38 |
| SIPES | 39 |
| THE LAST TRANSMISSION | 40 |

## III  THE FATHER CLOCK

| | |
|---|---|
| THE STOPWATCH GENE | 44 |
| THE PAST OUT FRONT | 45 |
| SMUDGED HAPPINESS | 46 |
| GENERATIONAL DEFENSE SYSTEM | 47 |
| ME VS EROSION | 48 |
| HIGH GRADING | 49 |
| THIXOTROPY | 50 |
| GRABBING GLOCHIDS | 51 |
| CREASES | 52 |
| MY FATHER OUTLAWED LOITERING | 53 |
| FLICK | 54 |
| BATHYMETRY | 55 |
| THE TIMEFRAME OF COMBUSTION | 56 |
| THE LIFESPAN OF A SUD | 57 |
| SLUMBERING THUNDERPLUMP | 58 |
| NOURISHMENT | 59 |

## IV  THE DIRT CLOCK

| | |
|---|---|
| PLENTY OF TIME | 62 |
| AUTOSTEREOGRAMS | 63 |
| GRABBING GUARANTEES | 64 |
| HALCYON STATIC | 65 |
| RETURN OF THE LANDLINE | 66 |
| THE ART OF TELLING TIME | 67 |
| REFUSING EXTINCTION | 68 |
| SHORT SEASONS | 69 |
| FROM BEHIND THE FERN | 70 |
| THE LAST DAYS OF ANGER | 71 |
| BECOMING AN ARSONIST | 72 |
| IMITATION PETRICHOR | 73 |
| EATING MY CHILDHOOD | 74 |
| SMELLING MUMS | 75 |
| THE FAR HOPE | 76 |
| FIGHTING TINY TIME | 77 |
| RINGS | 78 |
| ACKNOWLEDGMENTS | 81 |
| ABOUT THE AUTHOR | 83 |

# Time Billionaire
KG NEWMAN

"Asking myself the question, 'When I'm old, how much would I be willing to pay to travel back in time and relive the moment that I'm experiencing right now?'

"If that moment is something like rocking my six-month-old son to sleep while he hugs me, then the answer is anything: I'd literally pay all the money I'd have in the bank at, say, age 70 to get a chance to relive that moment. This simple question just puts things in perspective and makes you grateful for the experience you're having right now versus being lost in thoughts about the past or the future."

— *Muneeb Ali, Tribe of Mentors*

# I
# THE IDENTITY CLOCK

Give me everything in slow motion,
and underscored by a requiem score:
Amphora overflowing with Ibuprofen.
Things less complete than I always imagined
them to be. Something caught in
my throat while wondering about trees.
Me up in them. Testing skinny branches.
Fitting a spyglass from leaves, if only
I knew what direction to point it.

# FISTFULS OF GRAVEL BENEATH OUR FEET

Shrinkrays and barbed wire:
A porthole to view
requiems through

and the frying of time.
A son walking over the hill
amid mist and smoke.

What is forever if not
the bottling of the alpenglow?
The sowing of a long crop

that our grandchildren
trade for the ability
to stop the clocks when

streetlights blink, as if
carpeting the way toward
this detritus coalescing

into something we can
sit on, recline even,
watch sky scald the sun.

# THE WATCH WAR

When the sun comes up
I speedwalk backwards
to a tall cover crop.

Sprint with my wife
through a life cycle of corn
just to slow time.

Order doctors to
cut out my mind's
eighty-millisecond buffer
so now I see in pure azaleas
and dogwoods and

horses growing old
and breakable, sons
outgrowing gloves, meteors
flaming at random over
a weathered marbleyard

and an old man
sitting in the kitchen with
a gray dog at his feet
and bare wrists

and dawn streaking through,
daydreaming about
how long it takes
a fence post to split.

# TIME BILLIONAIRE

I took apart my watch and hid
the pieces around the house.
Walked through the park and
casually slid my phone into
a bear-proof trash bin. Taped
pictures of my two boys at their
weakest and strongest moments
to the bathroom mirror. To all the
mirrors. Until they weren't mirrors
anymore, just collage reminders
of the sand in my hands. It's like I'm
transferring the grains from one
bucket to another. So I keep my
fingernails long for this reason.
I slander the moment after sunset
in public. I walk down the street
screaming DEATH TO ELECTRICITY
when all I really want is to arrive
where the sidewalk meets the beach,
where I get a penny for every
second I have left and the billion
shiny copper circles stack into
an infinite oil rig, jacked up,
way out there in the ocean.

# OFF-DAY DEMANDS

Can I get a beeper again

smell mail with no return address

be a boulder of a man
who wears a lumberjack shirt
when it's winter out
and doesn't even think
about getting cold

Yes the text line is still a thing
No you cannot
have my email for the contest

I just want to be paged
I want green words rolling
across a slim black dial
on my waist saying

*The office is closed indefinitely*
*due to the snow squall*
*Your son grew back into*
*a baby and needs help*
*chewing his plastic keys.*

# THE FELLED PINE TREES SPEAK

I am the god of cabinets left open
and illegally picking wildflowers
and loves with too many commas.

Thus the opening for them
to slip war under the door
while I was wandering into
other people's photographs
and memorizing the bubble letters
of bar-stall autobiographies.

At least the certainty of anger
puts me to sleep each night
while the felled pine trees speak
even if no one notified their kin
of the char, and the beetles,

on a mountain made of mountains
where birds made of birds
flutter down to hand out a medal
for when my parachute
refuses to open as retribution
for hope, deceivingly blue
alpine lakes, glass-bottom boats.

So this is me now, silverware drawer
unorganized, dismantling my replicas
and wishing on stars that
are actually spaceships as I lick stamps
of famous dead-ball ballplayers
to stick between the pages
of my self-help books,

trying to figure out if this is
a forest fire or an infinite cigarette
hand-rolled to keep me warm because

it is winter and
no one asked me if I am ready.

# BLACKOUT

Oil tankers keep running ashore
as I sit on the beach
in a tub of ice, watching
the raptors take flight.
The bookies are sinking.
The language of winking
altogether forgotten.
It's not all math as we
are self-extincting ourselves.
Drinking the clepsydras dry.
Even futuristic sonar
won't save me. Just check
the EKG. The cloudless sky
and a flute somewhere
in the distance, trying
to revive the power plants.

# EASY TIME

Let the phone ring
and the election signs be
while our trolls
turn to technicolor dancers
and we remember
what a deep, dedicated
stretch feels like.
Blowtorching anger.
Rediscovering glitter.
The therapy of fur.
Whatever we potted and died
returning as something
unexpected next spring.
A black cactus.
Relentless optimism.
A tin umbrella
I dig up as a shield
or a thin gold watch
with a blank face and
a single worn button
that plays our son's laugh.

# RE-BEING PETER PAN

I am waiting for my son's laugh
to break into a thousand band-aids,
to patch the abscesses we can't fix.
Sure, we will still be standing
on the wrong shore.
And the winter wind
won't let us shake
the aching in our ears.
But maybe there's a dusty bodega
somewhere off the foot-tracked path,
selling already-lit smokes and
birds we could train
as mediators. They'll circle
a sun willing to accept
the role of the moon,
sans costume, high above a barn
dressed as a house, spiders cozy,
sons becoming young again,
a solitary blue fox attempting
to summon the equinox.

# THE SHEARING

I hold a push-up contest on the moon
and no one shows and
I still manage to lose so

I pull my beanie up to the tips
of my cauliflowered ears

collect the toy army men
from the dusty high-beams

and even with their guns
poking me through my pockets

I fall asleep on the hay-strewn floor
in that sad red barn
with a busted roof,
in the middle of a crater where

my secret identity is a frozen hydrant
somewhere in the forgotten city
plus the sheep I gave away
in a long-called-for exchange
for the return of the eves.

# IT'S OKAY EVERYTHING'S FINE

Weightless, I become seed
and sun at once. Terminal
sideways velocity, like a puff
of cotton. Escalating over
the crowns of the trees.
Infinitely editable. Incapable
of self-deprecating. I'm looking
for first-aid kits made of clay.
Or a collection of snake skins
I can retire off of. The higher
I get, the better I breathe.
The whiter the sky the more
I squint and exhale arrows
at my doppelgängers smoking
atop the silos of the moon.

# COTTONWOOD SUMMER

I stop fighting time
and lean into quickness:
Forget about Irish goodbyes
and I promised I wouldn't,
but did, look up
the drying time of cement.
I refuse to run. Trade apps
for a pack of feral pups
and put a premium
on shade over sunscreen.
So far their paws double-tap
every photo depicting
wrinkles and personal worsts
that I attach to the widest
and wisest trunks, as I
stop worrying about beetles,
as I count tree rings as
seconds float by as white
in a long-awaited breeze.

# SINGE ME

Within my thirty billion seconds left
I have other quantifiables i.e.
tens of thousands of moments
I choose not to look at clocks;
an estimated seventeen million
deep breaths; at least a couple
generations of trees I can see
from seed to firewood;
an unknown large quantity
of guaranteed smiles
and enough productive tears to fill
the truck tank for eternity
as the fear of the tick
becomes smoke and ash
in this hope bonfire.

# AMBROSIA FORMULA

Multiply my hustle to the elevator
by the accumulation of seconds saved from
two decades of California stopping,
times the time pocketed between thunder
and lightning while ripping into the drive
after a long day of work cut short,
divided by my son catching bugs after
the rain in muddy patches of the front
lawn, to the power of petrichor, squared.

# MY CRETACEOUS PERIOD

I want my life rewritten from a movie
into a *film* — to be fine with a slow drip
from casket spigots, the dog digging
under the fence, forgotten reservations,
time-thieving babies — and with the iconic
lines and contrails left over, I'll build
a rocking horse for my grandkids while
waiting for the meteor to flame in and
becoming a variation of a robot
cartoon dinosaur that is still
learning how to use his tiny arms.

# THE GALLOPING FIELDS

I blow off my expensive therapist and go
to the open fields by my house instead,

this after walking into the crowded grocery store
and right back out, admitting aloud to a passing old man

that I'm incapable of making these kinds of decisions today.
But the horses, who gallop through tallgrass and up

and down ravines with ease, they have no problem
knowing what way to cut through mud.

As I sit here with an ice cream tub melting in a bag
in my lap, I wish only that some dogs could join the horses,

and my vision also assumes 350 degrees as
I cannot see the weeds I'm eating in front of me.

I accept the thorny crunch. I believe I can drink
five gallons of water per day. Never vomit again.

I feel myself on my feet just after birth,
already putting all ten ear muscles to use,

sleep-standing with my third eyelids acting
as green screens, fit for whatever pasture, ever.

# FREEFALL

Snow slides off the barn roof as next summer remains
an oversized concrete eroteme, seeing as everything feels
like a jumping hour. I ignore the ice that stays stubborn
and the frosted cars piled up as carnage in the medians,
orange tags on their handles flapping in the wind.
Perhaps this is what it looks like when the fracking runoff
just can't go on with itself. Or it's punishment for being shirtless
through the August equinoxes. Anyways it's enough to make me
suddenly religious. Pickaxing the padlocked truth box.
The way I draw a stiff, frozen bow back like the toxophilite
of toxophilites, me being the clouds and the plane
moments before there ceases to be a sky at all.

# II
# THE HEART CLOCK

Upstate, before the cabin burned
down, before I decided between
being a fishmonger or a logger
or that I did my best work against
the ropes, I kept waking up a day
younger, seeing her sunglasses
on the dresser, working on
learning a chord she might
recognize from the early aughts.

I studied orbs on her shoulders
after getting out of the shower.
Planted a row of orange trees
west-facing, just to sketch
sun shading on her face. That was
before matches. Before I told her
Watch this, I got it, for us
I'll light this whole box at once.

# BECOMING WOODCHIPS

I'm tie-dye — I'm popping my neck —
I'm building more skylights and
doing recon on the country song
my wife's been humming

while I siphon the blue mortar
from the brick wall around
the house, for use for a future
chiminea. She keeps asking Where is

our quiet place? While I rev
the saw and declare the beauty
of deadwood, as if I ever saw us
as anything but fuel.

# OUR DE-EXTINCTION

Within the vivarium
the clock is a stalk of corn

and the grown sons
who don't know their
father's favorite beers
are assigned a paper route
in targeted neighborhoods.

Stretching is required
to unlock breakfast.

There's no need for
tonic immobility anymore.

Even the stores that
sell fake sun are falling
in line — recalibrating

the code between
need and want and
burning violet necessity,
the wives we almost lost
putting on lipstick again.

# MY PERSISTENCE OF MEMORY, EXPLAINED

There goes Dali again,
strolling through the Paris squares
with his anteater on a leash

while I think about how my wife
put her lipstick on, before she said
she was never in love

and the idea of us was
a struck fawn on the side of the road
for the crows to pick apart.

In the hanging-on paintings that remain
on our stained wallpaper
we are the whips of smoke

coming off my lips as I walk
into the house at dawn and hear only
steaming water streaming in the sink

where I imagine her washing ants off
a pocketwatch, about to Saran wrap
the camembert of time.

# OUR ETERNALISM

After trashing my watch
I dedicated myself to things
that make me lose track
of time: novels and golf

and blackened bacon we can
laugh about because we
were too busy singing to the baby
to see the smoke rising

from the forest, and the words
we knew but stopped from saying
worming themselves from
the earth, waiting for a boot.

# THE FRUIT MATRIX

I had a dream I was the red boy in the red chair
in the middle of the ice pond and older me
was a giant hacking away at the blocks
with a purple plastic hammer.

In the next chapter, where bricks met
carpet, I machine-gunned my demons
but due to a glitch they kept coming back bigger,
dressed in golden capes and diamond armets.

So I took over, lucidly, and timed
all the stoplights through town.
I waited out rush hour perfectly
just to save her, just in time to come home
and find our bedroom turned to a grove.

# TINY REPRIEVES

There's a goldfinch walking in the road
daring cars to brake.

Highways with faded yellow guardrails
cutting through selfish mountains
that want our dangerous love
all to themselves.

Hidden baseball fields
kept up by forgiving grazing goats
and water from ex-holy tarns.

On the way, we swerve around sweepers
with spinning splintered wire brushes
that make us think of couples therapy:

We're running from empty pantries.
Forest fires we may have started.
A green hydrant on the curb
by a graffiti'd downtown warehouse

and redacted versions
of National Geographic stacked
on end tables in relationship oncology
waiting rooms everywhere,
making us the numbest of numb
before figuring out what dinosaur
we can be for the kids and also
still come back as oil.

# BUNDLED TIME

We turn years into weeks
with three kids and
every sport we can afford.

Our cupboard features
fourteen blue water bottles
with broken or lost lids.

We dare the thick red gas line
on trips to the pass, pass on
oil changes, clutch anything that

gets us somewhere and could
also implode at any time.
There are wooden apples

on the backyard vine
beside a beetlekill tree playing
its accordion accordingly.

Every night I am left
humming its hits and
sweeping the bits of the day

into a cracked dustpan,
rearranging the bookshelf,
stapling pages to myself.

# THREADS

We live in an empty fish tank with stacks
of Scantrons with no wrong answers

and our son's old birthday invitations stuffed
in an overflowing envelope with

yellowed electric bills and other ephemera:
This following the era where we became

automation whose output is automata,
like an apology leads to sex,

and more backslide sex leads to a sheen,
which leads to green gas masks

to be worn during vigorous exercise.
We are scratching the walls. Spinning

around something. Wondering how long for
ombudsmen to burst through the door.

# COLLATERAL ORGANS

I agreed to the new-age lobotomy
that the nurse assured would erase
her snow prints on my brain
and the cruel syntax we used
to confuse morpheme with morphine.

When I went under I found myself
in a museum of canceled TV pilots
and the fee for entry was printing
all our son's portmanteaus
on a receipt streaming from my ear.

That's when I felt a jolt and heard
the burst of his laughter, years ago,
when he was small and our love
was big and the Edison bulbs strung
above the porch at cross-purposes.

In this new life the sky is bright
and the blubs are in a box somewhere.
The magic in the air turned out
to be WiFi, a bank account. Sprites
vaporizing the open cuts of us.

# ON MY MIND

A spark from dragging chains
can start a wildfire

A balloon is a type of ball
you can't have forever

Our quicksand vendor
is back in business
and I've developed an intimate
parasocial relationship
with a young Cameron Diaz

yet even with a green mask on
most days, I remain oddly specific about
parking spots and ice water

while perpetually searching my pockets
for my lost trombone
and Tommy gun.

I want to ask her when
it stopped being fun
but settle on another
weather observation instead.
Something about the giant white clouds

and how nothing could eat them gone
like they do each other.

# BURNING HANDS

The playlist is set
the corn is planted
the basketball courts
built in the center of
town with sterling silver
nets that rattle like a hymn
every time I sink one.

No need to reply to this
tableau, babe. I'll be here
working up a dark ring
on my hoodie, speed
dribbling, waiting for the
feeling of striking a fistful
of matches at once.

# SPORES

The house sounds are speaking to us
and telling me to look into purchasing
a jetpack, as I dream in the perspective of
dive-bombing ospreys. The relative location
of all fish-gremlins now moot seeing as
there is no longer a road or a pergola
to reference them by. We've drank
the lake dry and it's just fields now.
Beautiful women taking morning
dew baths. Me cementing my sleepmask
and remembering us through the force
of her handwriting, the cursive and
the roundhand, little lassos on letters,
enough slack on the line to tiptoe
way out over the chasm and time
how long for a penny to hit the bottom.

# ANNULUS

With our love expanding in concentric circles,
I stop thinking of truces and
half-zipped winter jackets, the crinkle
of two brown paper bags.
Of comets colliding and trains dictating
the time zones.
We could ride one out of here, sober,
whatever one rolls in next.
To where *undeniable*
is the only word that matters
and the atomic clock
is expected to neither gain nor lose a second
in a hundred million years.
Who knows what we'll be by then.
Martians. White dwarfs. The plastic
subdividers in our son's ant farm.
Possibly reincarnated
as those wandering ants
or ore-knuckled knockers who go around
to the monochrome hotel doors
of true, tired lovers,
making sure they somehow
wake back up for work.

# INFINITY TEA

Black and blue bricks, ground down
and sprinkled with

my son catching grasshoppers

rotted pillories
dotting the landscape
beneath copper windmills
the size of skyscrapers

A quincunx of stoplight poles
sharpened and spindling receipts
in my childhood intersection

to document how much time
we spend drinking water
and stepping around the center

Yes we are still testing the fans

and Sundays with unlimited toppings

trying to believe in chickens
riding vacuums and dogs
loading dishwashers

Cookie timers perpetually dinging

while I ignore the kitchen smoke
with a walk down a dirt road,
sipping, gulping,
taking a crusted wash cloth
and rubbing it fiercely against my knee
at the old bus stop,
recreating scrapes,

becoming a little vessel again.

# THE TAN LINES ON OUR WRISTS

We are not a watch, we are a horological machine:
Piano in the morning, whiskey at lunch.
Skeleton riding shotgun, drinking a cold one.
Anger begetting jazz and smoke bombs
in our server room, served with ice chips
in our interruptions. Why have we been
covering up the mechanisms?
How can we master the jump hours?
I told her I want to see her
as a dial floating, perpetually.
Us becoming the crossroads
of mechanics and art,
chronographs to keep us honest,
the alpenglow and antitwilight and minute repeaters
we need as we stumble through the dark.

# SIPES

I trace a quarter with my blood
and map out the squeaks in
the late-night floorboards.

I am hand-fighting skeletons
with tapers while relishing
the baby crying on my shoulder.

I turn myself off, and back on,
to stop smoking. Rotate my tattoos.
Take a toothbrush to my worn tires:

Bicycle, dinged truck, Lego ambulance
that rushes me deep into
the vortex of her hair where there

is running water, and light pillars,
beams waiting to be transferred
from one cut to another.

# THE LAST TRANSMISSION

Running with our garden
strapped to our backs,

our love becomes a stat graphic,
a tracking parabola,
either a leaking blimp

or floating poisonous pufferfish
from the craned perspective
of our tiny former selves
down on the ground.

We are chants we can't
recognize. Archipelago lost
to itself. Loitering sand

so annoying it reminds us
of something beautiful
like an hourglass on a string
spinning in the wind.

# III
# THE FATHER CLOCK

Up in the backyard skyfort with my sons
we tell time by the clouds
and how many juice pouches
we have left.

Bo, who just learned to sit,
grabs a sword by its blade
his hands immune as he chews
on the plastic edges
and multicolored Nerf bullets
with his two new front toofers.

Jax looks through the scope
down into the tall grass
and spots a bullsnake.
*Ka-pow!* goes his
battery-powered camo rifle
and a dirt puff kicks up
enabling temporary immunity
from clouds as we celebrate.

# THE STOPWATCH GENE

My father becomes gears
and during one of his
carefully scheduled visits
he whispers that
I'll inherit the clocks
plus his short-listed days,
the ripples in the river,
trees wearing trench coats
in heavy Colorado snow.
This without any

particular brokenness
in his tone and a cold
downtown deserted,
nothing too early except
in our expectations
of a difficult talk, maybe
late into the night, while
raccoons spill a trash can
and we pretend
to not hear a thing.

# THE PAST OUT FRONT

I can't stop this fear of dog years —

seeing the grandfather clock
as an elegant weapon —

I'm going mad imagining
the end of the tide while counting
a growing stack of onesies
that don't fit anymore,
a series of ascending trikes and bikes
clumped in the corner
of a dimly light garage
where I sit by the work bench
smoking and watching
the moths get high too…

This is how summer comes and cold
becomes a curse word

Why I always cut the lawn
with hand shears

Why I keep waiting for a bird to fly by
and turn back into a fledgling.

# SMUDGED HAPPINESS

*We need more flaws to make the memories perfect*
is what my grandfather used to say as he and I
mopped up the oil leaking from his rusting trusty truck.

This was shortly before the cancer called and we had
that reunion, where all the grandkids reenacted
a black box version of each major moment of his life.

When we went to take the cast photo with him,
he held the handmade blue playbill upside down. Hence
why I mop my garage; why when a rag soaks through

I pull it off the broom and enjoy replacing it from a stack
stretching high to the rafters, my blackened hands dusty,
my gaze waiting for an old gray mouse to scurry by.

# GENERATIONAL DEFENSE SYSTEM

My father was an aircraft carrier
sent to measure the dust
on the old oil fields.

All the empty jet slots
were filled with beer and
pallets of humidified pencils.

*I like how even aliens need armor*
he'd remark while flying
with a cigarette out the window

in one hand, and his other
cupping a stained-glass grenade
sitting in the middle console.

*The speed limit is erasable*
he'd also quip before revving it
through thick gray clouds,

cracking his neck as I pried
the reverse binoculars
free from my brow.

# ME VS EROSION

I stuff my son's leftover donut and the receipt from the mechanic
into the soup-can time capsule. Plus a couple cheap fortune slips
with forgotten worries scribbled on the back. As I'm burying it
next to my cactus in the side yard, Betty stops walking her cat
and asks if this is part of an ongoing documentary. I say yes.
That tomorrow I'm going to collect dandelion seeds and glue them
into a mosaic on the mailbox. Cut my son's hair and use it
to patch the grass in the front. Betty just nods and keeps on
walking her cat. I yell after her I REALLY WILL and then shove
my spade back in the black dirt, already expecting a clink
from the top of some treasure chest, or better yet, my son
suddenly toddling out the screen door, reversed to two again,
and ready to come up with another pseudonym for the wind.

# HIGH GRADING

I cry as I tie the brick atop my son's head. Make him guzzle coffee
in case the theory is true. Lie and say there are forty-eight hours in a day

while I keep a vial of the air from each vacation in my desk drawer,
for when my prayers lack a thesis as I seek the memory of a big tree

and purple sky rewinding. For when I'm begging for the forest
to restore itself to four stories, perpetually, as the timber industry

builds our house, his outgrown rocking horse, his pencils,
the mailbox filled with birthday cards every week it seems
and all that will remain if I don't stay focused with this string
are random, malformed saplings, swaying in the thin mountain wind.

# THIXOTROPY

Monday comes again
and with congratulations,
with fire in the kites
and lemongrass

on my skin. Maybe
I can use clone troops
for those proposals
or email my son's teacher
to see if she can get him
to repeat first grade.
As the synth escalates

how can I get time
to acc/decelerate?

I'll take a sack
of baby dragons
and release them
over the canyon.
Wedge myself

between two cliffs
fusing together,
shoot up the flare,
just to make sure
my son knows
where to meet me
on Tuesday.

# GRABBING GLOCHIDS

I become a purple cactus
wearing a beer hat
walking in a high desert
toward approaching snow.

Photosynthesizing in reverse.
Waiting to emerge
as a loved one's medicine.
Until then I try not to rot

as I pass through doors
at gas stations and distilleries
and infirmaries for
the emotionally broken

where I dream of a field of
the world's tallest cacti, and
adoration from a young boy
looking way, way up.

# CREASES

I pack the perfect snowball just to watch it melt in my hands
and then use that power to rub my son's back as he falls asleep.

This is winter on repeat. Soon these footie jammies won't fit
and it'll be summer, slipping through again, pushing against clouds

and that I have the smell of grass memorized. Lightning bugs in jars
with white sand floors and a paper top with holes poked in the shape

of a smiley. My son asks how long they will live but I am too busy
systemic dreaming to offer a response: Villas made of clouds.

Trees leaning downstream and me and my son walking the floodplain,
looking for a spot dry enough to lie down, become a paper airplane.

# MY FATHER OUTLAWED LOITERING

I stop worrying about my son graffitiing glass with his breath and tiny fingers:
this progress offset by my anger at the construction workers for a delay on the way

to school, a felony clock robbery, and as my son draws a stick dinosaur in the fog
I roll down my window and shout DEATH TO ROAD ROLLERS while wishing for

a smooth ride and simultaneously vibrating along a just-stripped lane, flattening cones,
my son looking at me, a blue sky, the future through a slightly askew rearview mirror.

# FLICK

The table plays a small game with the paper triangle. A touchdown, a field goal, an afterimage of myself hanging off the ledge. The rules are desperate dads in the wood-grass, with thumbs touching and pointer fingers to the sky. My heart is a turnover that is too late to change. The drop from top to carpet is the blink of early childhood. Arching kicks taunt the air. I wish I was more in the moment, I don't know. More like a yellow post that has met dirt. I'm half the desired time remaining on a frozen scoreboard; all evening I wait to get hit in the eye, twice, then I die to the sound of my son's uncapped laugh.

# BATHYMETRY

I only eat jolly ranchers
on clear fall afternoons, like if
my son brings two out in his palm
when I pick him up from school.

We'll suck them down
on the drive home and discuss
our plan to make aquanauts
relevant again. I'll convince him

it really is possible to measure
each trench to the centimeter.
Then we'll see how high he can
climb the pine out front, and if

it's too high, we'll figure out
a way for him to stay a while.
The rancher will be long dissolved.
We'll map oceans a different day:
There'll be time for the ticker
and simple lives later. Our priority
is now seeing how to get oxygen
down to the deepest deep.

# THE TIMEFRAME OF COMBUSTION

A watch cinched too tight
around my wrist and
a clocktower chiming the future:

This is why I sew a sundial onto each
of the striking pads
when training my son

when even the microwave timer
became SOFT or CRISP
as if digits were outlawed again:

*Not yet but soon*
my father would say over
a slow Friday night smoke

with some new, trendy moths
circling and seeking
their chance at self-immolation.

# THE LIFESPAN OF A SUD

Our world is bubbles and easily sunk tugboats.
The comforting slow drip from the faucet.

Me on the turtle stool, Bo discovering the sound
of a splash. It echoes off the tiles louder than

you'd think. Up towards where evening sun
is coming in the skylight. Slices of burnt orange

radiating… dare I say stalling? Definitely
at least trying to keep this water warm.

# SLUMBERING THUNDERPLUMP

My son lets his stuffies get dusty
in favor of snuggling two commemorative baseballs
when he goes to sleep: one black and one gold
from the local all-star game
the year before he was born, when I cut
the rainy derby short and rushed through traffic
to his mom in the hospital, pale and knocked out,
and the doctor told me in simple language
*There's been a miscarriage.*
I stood there stunned kind of like how
I'm rocking him now, but different, town of trees
achieving peak ecological succession-ish,
smelling the wisps of his just-washed little blond head
as he grips them tight, full-circle palm,
ready to throw the change when I fold up
my umbrella bat, and am sitting on the heater.

# NOURISHMENT

For breakfast I smooch my newborn
seventeen times. Lunch is a hug
with my son. For pre-dinner
I take my daughter to coffee,
hold my coffee. I'm more
of a water guy. Mix it
with the formula. Power the dam
that powers our house, where
I walk through on quiet afternoons,
just before school's out, before
daycare expires forever, turning on
lights in all the bedrooms.

# IV
## THE DIRT CLOCK

Memory supplements
and clogged water clocks.

Hourglass sand beneath
bare feet in the kitchen.

An orange tulip in
an oval terrarium in
a field of snow
and a billion seconds

stuffed deep in the freezer,
beneath the ice cream and

popsicles too cold to eat
without a little thawing.

# PLENTY OF TIME

I bend the wind and dream of the candelabra era.
Subways always running on schedule.
Cement mixers collecting dust
because fields in the city are protected for dogs,
infinite fetch. In this utopia I have
a little one on my lap, a son perpetually young and
speaking in the most beautifully organic portmanteaus.
Cowboots. Firecrackerworks. Hamwiches for days.
The firens blazing after an accididn't yesternight
when the wax spilt all over the kitchen floor
and dried in the shape of a jellyfish.

# AUTOSTEREOGRAMS

The whole year was a grift.
Broken small talk and umbrellas
with microscopic holes.

Charcuterie boards made of
thin sticks and pain pills.
Glitching memories. Locomotives
filled with jelly. Straightjackets
for everyone. Watches buried

in boxes all along the beach.
Seizures masquerading
as dancing. Imphepho freezing
under a match that lights
the way down a tunnel
to the middle of the sky:

From up here, I can hear
the universe straining
to open and close again,
hypnotized by empty grocery carts
abandoned by yesterday.

# GRABBING GUARANTEES

Up on the ridge, where I judge
the longing by the length of light,
a whitetail deer licks graffiti boulders
as the sun fades on another day.

A truck backfiring echoes from
the road below. What I want is
the sunset and the shotgun sound
rolled into a joint that the deer
helps me spark. After we start
feeling lucid and relax amid

the feather reeds, darkening clouds
look like gears disappearing and
the sands of an hourglass spilling
onto the horizon, ready to be
scooped up in the morning,

converted to gravel, used to build
a path back to a garden where I can
always assume something's in bloom.

# HALCYON STATIC

When the applesauce pouches run down
in the last days of the kingdom of nil
the space between hilltops and clouds
is an echo chamber for prayers

received as surrender. Dead fish
float downstream and kids take tests
with pencils without erasers while

in the weeds behind the blood factory,
minotaurs on oxygen are desperate
to solve Rubik's Cubes. There is no
deflecting reflections on sidewalks
strewn with shattered cobalt glass.
There are only sad people driving

with just enough gas to accept
the decisions they've made as they
daydream of a bird nesting
at sea, what its lifespan is,
and how high the waves will be
when it decides to fly away.

# RETURN OF THE LANDLINE

People forgot about the blinking red dot
but I did not, not after
I threw my smart phone in the fireplace
and stood on the front lawn,
waiting for the bishops of the world
to celebrate the white smoke.

This disconnect became
my religious experience, after
the apps, cracked screens
and trite quests for lost chargers
that were our aluminum divinity.

Now my only obsession is when
I walk through that door after a long day
of natural struggle: Breathing exhaust
on the crosswalks, imagining an island
while the boss rages, sneaking a spliff
in the alley on lunch. Yet never
a rectangle to check. Not in the office

or the drive home during rush hour.
It's just me and the radio, cutting
in and out, then later the anchor
telling me the bad that happened
that afternoon, the small bits of good too,

the bishop saved by the vagrant
from drowning in the river,
the river the schoolchildren
worked all fall to unpollute

so it could run free again
down to the sea where the air
vibrates at frequencies only an ear
pressed to a shell can hear.

# THE ART OF TELLING TIME

My baby speaks in rawrs
and his currency is bubbles.

Proof the prehistoric
can jive with the fleeting.

This is why I banish
alarms in our house

and write a formal letter
to the school board asking

for clock-reading to be
stricken from the curriculum.

My wife says this is worse
than my brick-and-string theory

to keep the kids of the earth
from growing tall and jaded

and I say just wait until
I campaign against waiting and

use sand from county hourglasses
to fill in the infield nicks:

This is where the stegosaurus
will re-emerge from dirt, redefining

fossil as a thing to lay down on
and watch the stars gas out.

# REFUSING EXTINCTION

My whole life is light-up dinosaurs
and turning clocks around.

Picking which whisper to listen to
while walking down infinity halls,

burying fossils atop warped walls
for the son of my son's son. In history

he will learn about taxis and why we
should've stopped at the flip phone.

And maybe he too will be obsessed
with restoring beauty from the dead.

He might even break at a café terrace
and feel no need to document it.

He will just sit there, sip his coffee,
watch two magpies fight over

a dropped slice of bread and then
bike home to his farm where

he collects eggs and carefully cleans
the coop of his own dinosaurs.

# SHORT SEASONS

The average cloud lives for four minutes
before dissolving into a baby dinosaur

whom I arm-bar for
the last prehistoric fern.

All while running cemetery stoplights,
a thumbtack short and a couple hugs late,
speeding to recoup my long-lost yawns.

Later, leaf blower in one hand,
I boil regret with the other,
stirring, praying for my ears to pop.

Soon, with a split lip, I'll be
a chipped lamp in the far corner
of Goodwill. A stray dog pawing at

a warm back door where white trees
rise high above the houses, cutting down
on how much I have to shovel.

# FROM BEHIND THE FERN

the kneeling green army man
radios his sadness to the moth
lingering above the chandelier.
*Fear of emptiness is what we
make it,* added the porcelain tiger
sitting half-off the mantel ledge

all while I still waffle on which
whisper to listen to, turning my hat
backwards then forwards then
backwards again, pretending

I don't know myself and that
there's no need to apologize,
or lie, or stack pennies from
the counter to the ceiling just to
believe the unlikely backstory
to each found Lincoln might
bring a moment of contentment.

# THE LAST DAYS OF ANGER

I built a prison out of stacked pennies
and then built a wall around the prison
just to graffiti it and then

I tightened the tourniquet,
filled the tank, became the bird
lifting off the highway
seconds ahead of the semi tires

because it becomes blissfully simple
at the end, the water tower
emptied, the sky folded up and
forgotten in my wing pocket.

# BECOMING AN ARSONIST

I'm polishing the bar top after close,
taping my bat handles the night before,
perpetually smearing war paint on my face.

*They'll see* becomes something to see:
dogpiles with my sons, maximizing art,
minimizing emailing. Simultaneously

grabbing the light side of fire. Eating
just asparagus tips. Self-actualizing as
a time billionaire, damn the suggested

philanthropy: We're burning everything
now, we're eating the mangos. I'm dialing
my infant's four-inch foot phone

to call it in, like a brush fire inhaling
momentum: White ash twirling as I sit
on my porch, smoking formaldehyde.

# IMITATION PETRICHOR

The future's not as glitzy as we imagined —
It's a fat old man in a tattered veteran's cap
smoking a menthol cigarette and
wearing a yellow poncho,
bending gingerly with his cane
for a packet of mayonnaise lying
on the wet curb at the bus stop where
he waits for nothing but clouds

and a storm that passed decades ago,
as did the girl who used to
carry a stack of bright books
under her arms as she walked
around 14th's puddles, wishing she'd
believe in birds again or at the least
be someone's arsonist to light
the city's haberdasheries on fire.

# EATING MY CHILDHOOD

The ants went marching into hell
and Old Mac is foreclosing on his farm.
Between evil laughs
a reconstructed Humpty Dumpty acknowledges
it's grim, uncertain times with
Moby Dick washing ashore riddled with spear holes
while Mocha Dick reincarnates, and
all the dads' rear views fall off, and
kids grow up cussing in metered nursery rhyme.
*This is the irreversible*, Humpty says between
long drags of his cigarette, and before
scaling the water tower to tag it up,
then siphon off a bit of blood sunset.

# SMELLING MUMS

When the black fox
comes to our village
with a quiver filled
with chrysanthemums,
speaking of the
sacrifices made and
the sweat yet to be
culled, we greet him
with saxophones
and an air show.
The contrails paint
the future and

symbolize the endurance
he hopes his blind pups
inherit. Meanwhile,
my youngest son
climbs the highest tree
in the kingdom
to calculate
the true length
of a day. He is
to report his findings
to myself and the fox
at first alpenglow:
He knows this is the
only remaining way
to understand time.

# THE FAR HOPE

It's why I keep watering the wilting mums
every morning. Finding books
I'm not looking for. Why I can't just say
what's going on right now.
There's a couple kissing at the red light

proving it's not all that difficult.
Maybe I need to re-check
the extinction list first. Maybe the recipe
is less screen time and more
interesting animal facts. Mirror neurons.
Staying focused with an infant crying

in my hands. Becoming the old man
who can identify trains by whistle signals.
The same one with an overstuffed wallet
that takes an exercise to dig out
from the back pocket at the diner
where grandkids clamor for milkshakes.
It's why I keep watering the wilting mums

every morning and sometimes more
when I feel good in the afternoon, too,
in between writing the orbs and
dreaming of taking my sons on a jet,
scheming between contrails for my opening
to get us a few milliseconds younger.

# FIGHTING TINY TIME

A solar flare destroys the 24th hour
while an ancient eel swims through
a decaying reef and I keep falling
asleep at my desk. A tablet

dissolves in a glass of black.
A few less pages get read.
Leftovers are now just another bite
or two, muscle mass to be
added as distraction's subtracted:

Cell towers felled as blighted pines.
Can we keep the atomic clock
in a half nelson? The kids are
growing and some of them
die. So let's drill this again. Engines

sputter and soon the barber's floor
will be covered in gray clippings.
I'm singing to keep the moon away,
I'm holding its head underwater
with one hand and throwing my

achy fist at the immortal jellyfish with
the other, desperate to get stung
like a first stylet flooding back
or, in best case, the original bee.

# RINGS

The city makes me for a splinter
and an approximate solitaire.

It cements me within
the half-life of a decaying stadium
where someone in the rotunda dons
unsuspecting statues with scapulars.

My sins written in chalk
on all walkways orbiting
the riverfront, with not a cloud in sight.

Sons learning to ride bikes in cul-de-sacs
projecting on the white sides
of high rises at twilight, like drugs
dissolving on the tip of my tongue

and the flags are at half-mast
and I have no idea why
other than to guess the factories must be
sleeping without dreaming again.

This is the place I pick
to save the prior minute's version
of myself: The pennies scattered
in a mirage off in the distance
and if I squint long enough,
they take the shape of a sequoia.

# ACKNOWLEDGMENTS

*The Watch War* first appeared in *Stone Circle Review*

*Time Billionaire* first appeared in *Thimble Literary Magazine*

*Singe Me* first appeared in *Blood & Bourbon*

*The Fruit Matrix* first appeared in *Timber Journal*

*Tiny Reprieves* first appeared in *Roi Fainéant Press*

*The Stopwatch Gene* first appeared in *One Art Poetry*

*Bathymetry* first appeared in *Trampoline Poetry*

*Nourishment* first appeared in *Erato Magazine*

*Plenty of Time* and *Refusing Extinction* first appeared in *Welter Magazine*

*Autostereograms* first appeared in *Ink & Marrow*

*The Art of Telling* time first appeared in *Mikrokosmos Journal*

*The Last Days of Anger* first appeared in *The Shore*

*Rings* first appeared in *MoonLit Getaway*

# ABOUT THE AUTHOR

**KG NEWMAN** is a Colorado poet and sportswriter for *The Denver Post*. His first four collections of poems are available on Amazon and he's been published in hundreds of literary journals worldwide. The Arizona State University valedictorian is on Twitter @KyleNewmanDP and more info and writing can be found at kgnewman.com. He is the poetry editor of Hidden Peak Press and the fourth-generation native of the Centennial State lives in Hidden Village, Colorado, with his wife, three kids and four dogs. When he's not writing or reporting, he can be found playing men's league baseball with his buddies on Sundays, golfing around his property, camping, skiing or coaching Little League baseball, basketball and football. He dreams in words, the projector long broken. And he's still waiting to paint the perfect poem.